Le
Wi

And \ , ·earns Are
Not Always the Answer

James Lawrence

CPAS Leadership Principal

GROVE BOOKS LIMITED

RIDLEY HALL RD CAMBRIDGE CB3 9HU

Contents

CPAS is an Anglican evangelical mission agency working mainly in the UK and Republic of Ireland. We enable churches to help every person hear and discover the good news of Jesus Christ. Our vision is to see effective, Christ-like leaders at all levels in our churches: men, women and young people who point others to Jesus. Good leadership is key to church growth and that is why we are investing all our energy in developing leaders.

www.cpas.org.uk.

Acknowledgments

Thanks to all those who have shown me the wonder of collaboration; too many to name, but all known to him.

First Impression April 2020

ISSN 2041-0972

ISBN 978 1 78827 120 2

1 Introduction

If I could gift every leader one thing, a great experience of genuinely collaborative leadership would be high on my list. I am very fortunate; throughout my time as a leader I have been privileged to be a part of some exceptional leadership groups.

As a curate my training incumbent treated me like a colleague despite my youthfulness (24) and lack of experience. We shared leadership with two members of the congregation and it was a fun and fruitful time.

As part of Springboard I joined a team of people from different theological traditions and learnt how to lead well with others as part of a national organization under an excellent ex-diocesan secretary.[1]

At CPAS I have been part of numerous different groups where we have tried to work out what shared leadership looks like, and have seen the wonderful benefits of a group of people working well together on a range of complex things.[2]

I have seen the wonderful benefits of a group of people working well together

However, I do not think I am a naturally collaborative leader (you will find out more about this later), but I have learnt the benefits of leading well with others and try my best to do so in any context I am in. As I said, I am fortunate.

Others are less so. Their experience of shared leadership is negative, perhaps one of the worst experiences of their life. For when it does go wrong, and sadly it does, it is terrible, putting you off any idea of collaborative leadership at all.

Or maybe it is simply a lack of any experience of shared leadership. They have not had an opportunity to lead with others and do not really know what it might look like.

If your experience matches one of the latter two categories I wish I could wave a magic wand and wipe the past away and give you an experience of great shared leadership, but I cannot. Instead, may I invite you to acknowledge what has been and ask God to help you temporarily set it aside. Then see whether there is a vision for leading well with others that can catch your heart and mind, and fire you with a desire for the potential of what good collaborative leadership might involve.

Leading well with others is both an attitude and a set of skills. The attitude can be adopted, and whilst for some that might be more of a challenge than for others, it can be done. The skill set can be learned through study, exposure to those who are good at collaborative leadership, and experience. Hopefully this booklet will go some way towards shaping both.

- Chapter two explores four aspects of leadership today that play into our experience of leading well with others.
- Chapter three identifies theological and pragmatic reasons why leading well with others is not an optional extra, but needs to be central to our understanding and praxis of Christian leadership.
- Chapter four offers a definition of what we mean by collaboration and identifies who we might collaborate with.
- Chapter five suggests ten tips for fostering a collaborative culture where new leaders are developed, and those already in leadership are encouraged to lead well with others.

2 The State of Play

Approaches to leadership change over time. Different approaches are emphasized, new ideas develop and expectations shift. It is part of what makes leadership complex, perhaps especially so in our time. In order to explore how to lead well with others, I want to outline four aspects of leadership today that affect the current state of play.

1 The Shift to a More Collaborative Way of Leading

Collaborative leadership is something of a buzzword. In interviews for leadership roles, if the panel ask, 'What is your style of leadership?' there is only really one acceptable answer: 'Collaborative.' Imagine someone saying 'Authoritarian,' 'Directive' or 'Pacesetting'; all styles of leadership identified through style surveys in the past. There would probably be a slight intake of breath.

Eighty years ago, the situation was somewhat different. Those born as part of the traditionalist generation (1925–1945) expected leaders to lead the way, to give teaching and direction, caricatured as, 'This way, follow me.'[3] Then came the baby boomer generation (1946–1963), where expectations of leaders began to shift as part of the post-war management era. People expected leaders to be professional, competent, to have letters after their names. Generation X (1964–1980) were not so keen on being told what to do and wanted leaders who would consult and understand them. They were followed by Generation Y or the Millennials (1980–2000) who expect leaders to collaborate and involve them from the start. They do not simply offer leaders respect because they have a title or a role, but offer respect when it is earned through healthy engagement. These are obviously generalizations based on generational typology,[4] but they helpfully reflect a shift in the approach to leadership that has occurred through the twentieth century.[5]

From a Heroic Individual to a Community of Leadership

It is less about a lone ranger operating on their own, a charismatic builder, and more about the leader as an architect working with others.

From Guarded to Vulnerable

In the past leaders were encouraged to be strong, not reveal weakness or fear; not to be vulnerable. I was brought up as part of this generation, where 'Men don't cry,' where if things get difficult you tough it out. However, Millennials were brought up in a different context, where expressing emotion and feelings was encouraged. One of the touchstones for this generation is authenticity and one of the ways they gauge this is through vulnerability. Therefore, it has been a quite a challenge for me to work out what appropriate vulnerability looks like as a leader who wants to connect with Millennials.[6]

From Positional to Earned Authority

Trust is not a given because of title, position, qualification or length of service, but is earned through relationship, compassion, care and competence. 'Because I said so…' will not get leaders far today. Instead, authority is earned over time.

From Task to Community

It is not so much about a task-focused approach where community is a by-product of getting something done, but rather community being the key to accomplishing a task. It is partly reflected in Millennials seeing fun as an important part of a working environment, building on their experiences of learning in early life. Leaders who do not invest in the culture of an organization alongside the vision are less likely to attract younger people.[7]

From Directing to Empowering

Rather than a command and control approach, leadership is more about cultivation and co-ordination. Common metaphors for leaders today include gardener and conductor, reflecting a more empowering dynamic.

From Aspiring to Inspiring

It is less about personally aspiring to higher levels of leadership and more about inspiring others to fulfil their potential. When younger leaders join an organization they are keen to know how they will be invested in from an early stage. They look for developmental opportunity.

These shifts in approaches to leadership are generally positive, although a wise leader knows how to draw on the whole spectrum of possible ways to lead. Sometimes a directing style is needed, or being guarded is sensible. In addition, whilst these are shifts that reflect a change in people's expectations across the generations, it does not mean there are not people out there who want leaders to lead in the old paradigm. There are, and plenty of them. This is what makes leadership so complex today, especially if you are leading in a cross-generational context.

2 Confusion over Terms

The second issue in the leadership landscape is considerable confusion over what we mean by collaborative leadership. Some think that delegation is collaboration. They work hard to delegate, and deploy, support and train those they delegate to in the best possible way. This is good, but delegation can happen without real collaboration taking place.

A leader told me how they enjoyed a collaborative approach to their work. I was intrigued and asked what that looked like. 'It's great,' he said. 'Over the years I've developed a group of people around me who I've delegated all the tasks to that I didn't enjoy or wasn't very good at. I can now concentrate on what I do well.' It certainly sounded good, but I was not convinced it was collaborative leadership.[8]

Others think collaborative leadership is about gathering others around them and empowering everyone to have an equal say in what happens. In this scenario, no one is 'the' leader, and anyone can take the lead. Again, this might work out well, but I am not sure it is necessarily collaborative leadership. It is far too easy for the loudest voice to dominate, for the strongest personality to get their way and for leadership to become anything but collaborative.

Others will use the language of teams, and suggest that a team is crucial for collaborative leadership. Yet even this is not as clear as we might like, since people have very different understandings of what a team is and how it might operate.

If we are to make progress in leading well with others, we need a clear understanding of what we mean and how it relates to a variety of things, in particular collaboration, teams and delegation.

3 Diversity of Contexts

Over the last 20 years CPAS has run a leadership course for younger church leaders aged 25–40. In the early days of this 18-month programme we ran modules on team building, and they worked really well for some but not for all. We decided to find out why.

What we discovered was that the leaders were coming from a wide variety of contexts. Some were in larger churches where there was a significant staff team of paid people working together. They met regularly, worked on projects together, shared life together.

Others were in medium-size churches where there was only one other member of staff, but often a core group of leaders who were involved in oversight of various ministry areas in the church. They tended to meet less frequently, worked on their specific areas, reported to the larger group and spent less time with those in that group. Finally, others were in smaller church contexts where they were the only paid member of staff; often part-time with a shortage of other leaders, if any at all. Frequently there were multiple congregations with less than 20 people in each, and even some of the legal structures were struggling to find people to be involved, for example on the PCC or deacon's group.

The team-building modules connected well with those in the larger churches and to an extent with those in the medium churches, but rarely with those in the smaller church contexts. It did not make sense of their reality.

In our wider work across the Church of England we have found this diversity of contexts replicated around the country. There are clergy who would like to collaborate but are struggling to find a way of making sense of this in their context, especially if the language of team is used.

On the Arrow programme, we decided to change our emphasis from building teams to leading well with others. This approach suggested that whatever context the leaders found themselves in, there was always a way to lead well with others, because in every context there are certain things in place that mean there are others around, even if others might mean just one person.

4 Lack of Ability (or Willingness) to Collaborate

Some years ago a colleague joined us at CPAS having worked for many years in a highly collaborative environment. After seven years working with Anglican clergy and in churches around the country, I asked him for his observations. His response was fascinating. He suggested that in his experience clergy generally talk a good game of collaboration, but in practice actually struggle to be collaborative.[9] It resonated with me for two reasons.

First, I know how difficult I find it to be genuinely collaborative. Like many of my generation, I was brought up with phrases like, 'If something needs to be done, do it yourself.' Whilst I believed theologically and pragmatically in the importance of leading well with others, I struggled with the reality of actually doing it. Secondly, working with leaders on Arrow and in other contexts, I had observed that I was not the only one struggling to be collaborative. The tendency to control things is perhaps part of what gets many people into leadership positions. Giving up that control is not easy. It is risky, time consuming, and requires both faith and trust.

Collaboration certainly sounds like a good thing, the right thing even. But being collaborative may not be as easy to do as it is to say. And there are some who do not even want to be collaborative. They are quite happy to be 'the' leader, quite happy to do things on their own, quite happy to keep things as they always have been.

It is in the context of these four realities that we explore why a collaborative approach to leadership might be crucial and what such leadership might look like.

3 The Case for Collaboration

Ours is an individualistic culture. No surprise, then, that for most of us the word 'leadership' prompts a mental picture of a person in charge—singular, not plural. But for theological and pragmatic reasons I want to suggest that leadership is plural, that leaders are best developed, and leadership best exercised in community. The consequences of not taking this approach are all around for us to see.

The Tale of Sally

Once upon a time there was a church leader called Sally.[10]

Sally arrived six years ago to find the church struggling with a stack of problems: high debt, low morale, no children or young people, small congregation and traumatic fallout from a pastoral crisis in the recent past. Some of the congregation were suspicious of Sally. Others quietly hoped she would be their saviour. Fortunately, Sally was certain that this was where God wanted her to be; she loved the job and the people from day one.

Sally poured herself into the life of the church, getting to know people, prayerfully discerning a new direction, working hard to enable action and caring for everyone she met. In the first year there were small, encouraging signs of change, boosting the congregation's level of expectation. By her second year financial giving was rising, a new service had started and people felt cared for. And though a few doubters remained, many people now thought that Sally really was their saviour.

By year three things were buzzing. But, of course, the more Sally did, the more work there was to do. The more she reached out within the community, the more there were to be reached. The more she started new things, the more things needed continuing. The more she visited the sick, the more unwell people there were expecting a visit. The more the budget increased, the more money needed finding.

Not surprisingly, by years four and five Sally was struggling. Facing exhaustion, she knew she could not continue as things were. And yet everything was going well in the church—her supervisor spoke warmly of what she had achieved. But Sally knew that work at this pitch was not sustainable. She started looking at job advertisements in the church press. In year six, she left to take up a new post.

What Went Wrong?

The seeds of Sally's situation were sown before she arrived at the church. She described her sense of call to ordination as a call to 'ministry.' She was trained to be 'the minister,' both on her course and during her previous post as an assistant minister. It led her to think that she was responsible for the ministry of the church, rather than seeing herself as the catalyst to enable the ministry of the people of God in the church. The template on which she based her ministry was that of the solo leader. Alongside this pattern of ordained ministry that shaped her approach to her role was the internal stuff that meant she feared two things. First, not succeeding; had not her supervisor said something about this being the last chance for the church? And secondly, losing control. Her training minister had constantly stressed the importance of knowing exactly what was going on in every aspect of a church's life, of being present at all the meetings and of ensuring all decisions were made by her.

It did not have to be like this. If only Sally had realized that Christian leadership is a corporate, shared community enterprise and rarely a solo performance.

A Theological Basis for Leading Well with Others

There is a significant transition from the Old Testament to the New Testament in the understanding of leadership. In the Old Testament God anoints individuals to lead: Deborah, David and Daniel come to mind. Called by God, he equips and empowers them by his Spirit to lead his people. In the New Testament that same Spirit is now poured out on all the people of God (Acts 2.17–21)—young and old, women and men, slaves and free, Gentile and Jew—to set them free, adopt them into the family of God and equip them to serve the purposes of the kingdom (Gal 3.26–29). Some of those who serve will serve as leaders within the body, and part of the role of the leaders is to equip God's people for works of service (Eph 4.11–13).[11]

As part of this transition from Old to New Testament, we discover leadership is plural—the majority of the references to leadership in the New Testament are in the plural. Theologian Gilbert Bilezikian comments, 'Throughout the New Testament, church leadership is presented as a collective ministry. Even when the indefinite term "leader" is used in the context of Christian community, it receives a plural reference (Heb 13.7, 17).'[12]

Why is this? The New Testament's main metaphor for the church is the human body, emphasizing the interdependent, communal aspects of many parts making a whole (1 Corinthians 12–14). Each part needs the other parts in order for the body to function well. Those in leadership are not separate from the body, somehow outside or above it (see Diagram 1). They are not exercising ministry for the body or on behalf of it; rather they are part of the body under the authority of the rightful head, Jesus (Col 1.8). Leadership is distributed throughout the body in a variety of ways (Diagram 2.)

Some exercise leadership in non-formal ways. They do not have a role, but nonetheless their influence is clear and shapes the life of the church. Some exercise their leadership in the Monday to Saturday life of the church dispersed throughout homes, community, schools and places of occupation. Some are called to take on a specific role of leadership within the gathered life of the church to help the body function well, for example as a leader of the children's group, the choir or an outreach project. Some are called to authorized roles of leadership (AL); recognized and trained by the wider church.

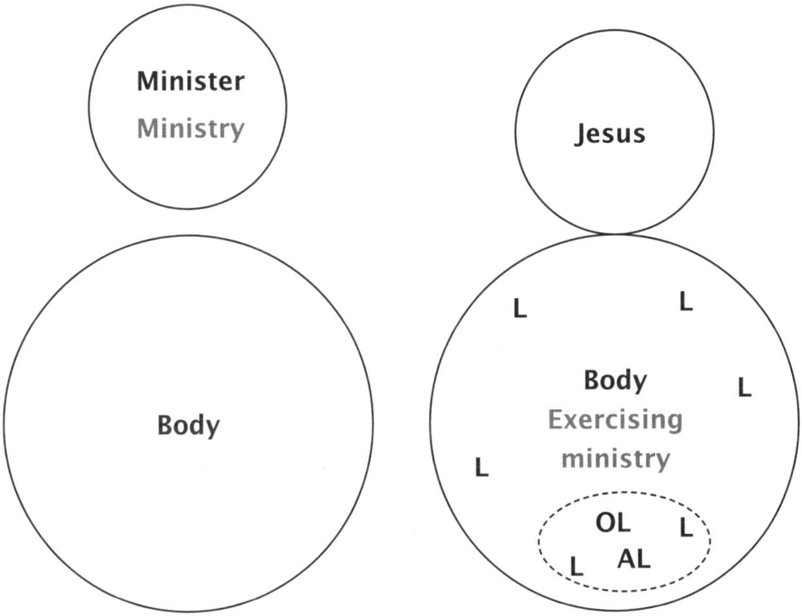

Diagram 1 Diagram 2

What is clear is that, whilst the ordained leader (OL) has particular responsibilities, part of which is to animate the people of God to be about God's mission and ministry, they are expected to share their leadership with others (hence the little group of leaders gathered in the dotted area in diagram 2). This is the pattern of the New Testament, where Paul models this in his own leadership (26 times he speaks of his co-workers) and encourages a plurality of leadership in the churches he writes to.

Theologically, this emphasis on leadership as a communal enterprise reflects the nature of the church as a body, which in itself reflects the nature of who God is. God is Trinity: Father, Son and Holy Spirit in relationship with one another. The communality of the Godhead is breathed into the life of the church as it seeks to live out the 'one anothers' of the New Testament, and is expressed in the way leadership is to be exercised amongst God's people.[13]

Another biblical scholar, Gordon Fee, argues that Western Christians struggle to see the reality of what the New Testament is saying on this issue because of the tension between individual and corporate life. 'Western Christians in particular are trained from birth to value the individual above the group, whereas in the New Testament perspective the community is still the primary reality, and the individual finds identity and meaning as part of the community.'[14] He suggests that rather than the clergy being a separate group from the laity, the leaders were simply an identifiable part of the whole people of God.

So the nature of the church (the body) reflects the nature of God; people in community mutually dependent on one another. And the nature of leadership reflects the nature of the church; a collective leadership that recognizes the need for people to lead in community.

A Pragmatic Basis for Leading Well with Others

Three statements capture well the practical reasons for leadership in community.

No One Leader Has All the Gifts Necessary for Leadership

Research consistently shows that even the most talented leaders do not have everything required for effective leadership. The Gallup organization's work in this area indicates that all leaders are limited, with the best leaders having just half the gifts needed for effective leadership.[15] To be honest, we do not need the research. I only have to reflect on my own life for a moment to realize how limited I am in my leadership. Clearly, for effective leadership, it helps if people share it with us so that we complement one another, bringing different skills, gifts, talents, passions, knowledge and experience.

No One Leader Can Possibly Do All the Leadership Required in a Growing Church

In a small church (and if you only have one congregation) it may be possible for the minister to do everything. 'Possible,' though, does not mean healthy. As we saw with Sally's story, it may set up patterns of ordained ministry and expectations amongst the congregation that are hard to change further down the track. However, if a church grows there quickly comes a point where the growth is limited by the time and abilities of the leader. The minister can become the proverbial cork in the bottle. It is not good for them, and it is not good for the church. A highly competent leader can make the mistake of disempowering members of the congregation who feel they are less able.

No One Leader Can Handle the Complexities of Church Leadership

I came across some research many years ago that identified the three most challenging contexts in which to exercise leadership. I was fascinated to discover that leadership in a local church was one of the top three.[16] Fascinated but, on reflection, not surprised. Leading a church is tough. The weight of the role is not insignificant, and the expectations hugely varied. The variety of skills required is enormous, from the managing of often ancient and burdensome buildings to the tricky navigation of multi-hat roles and relationships. The handling of a primarily volunteer workforce is complex and the engagement with an increasingly alien culture challenging. The list could go on. Such complexity demands a level of experience, knowledge, wisdom, perspective and skill that can only come from a group of people.

Thus, for theological and practical reasons, leadership is best exercised with others. Whilst this may not always be possible, I suggest it should always be the goal. From the outset it would have helped if Sally had seen—or been encouraged to see—the identification, development and deployment of others as leaders as one of her key priorities, and had the long-term aim of growing around her a small group of other leaders to join her in sharing leadership of the church together. For that to happen well she needed to be clear about terms and conditions.

4 Terms and Conditions

If leading well with others is a goal of healthy leadership, how might we best describe such an approach to fostering collaboration?[17] And with whom are we seeking to be collaborative?

Defining Collaboration

There are many ways of trying to define collaboration within a Christian context, each with their own strengths and weaknesses. I define it as follows, without claiming this is the correct definition; rather, a working definition for this book.

> Recognizing that we seek to join in with what God is doing, and that leadership is best exercised with others, collaboration is the action of working interdependently with others in a mutual, caring and complementary way towards a shared kingdom-honouring goal.

First, this definition notes that our primary collaboration is with God. Jesus is the head of the church. As such, we do not get to determine why the church exists; he does. So, our collaboration is first and foremost with what Jesus wants for his church and this local congregation of the people of God. The great commandment (Matt 22.34–40) and the great commission (Matt 28.16–20) certainly steer us clearly towards some of his priorities, as does his own statement of purpose in John 10.10, 'I have come that they may have life, and have it to the full.' For example, a church that is not concerned about mission, about helping people discover abundant life in Christ, is a church that is not collaborating with Jesus. When we seek to discern what to give attention to in the life of a church, we determine to seek God and his priorities at this time. It is why prayer and study of the Scriptures are such an important part of leadership life.

Secondly, it recognizes that collaboration is an action, a choice we have to make. Some of us are naturally collaborative, many of us are not. We will need to make a choice, a choice to work differently from perhaps our natural tendency. A choice based on a belief that this is the best way of working, even if it has not proved to be in the past.

Thirdly, the words 'interdependently,' 'mutual' and 'complementary' all hint at a critical factor in collaborative leadership. This is a way of working that is beyond delegation, a way of working that gives equal voice to all, embraces diversity, and believes that only together can we make the wisest decisions possible around the complex and weighty issues before us. There is a sense in which you do not need collaborative leadership when things are relatively minor and simple. Choosing the colour of the church coffee cups is simple and minor. Someone should be given the delegated responsibility to make that decision on behalf of others. But deciding what to focus the life of a church around over the next five years, that is a complex and weighty task that we would be foolish to allow one person to determine.

Such mutuality does not mean there is not a *primus inter pares*, a Latin phrase that means first among equals. The minister does have some unique responsibilities. There is a sense in which the buck does stop here. Part of the leadership aspect of their role is to take responsibility. That will mean many things: for example ensuring direction for the future is discerned; creating a safe and conducive environment for honest, robust disagreement; making a tough decision that carries significant consequences; leading the leadership group. But to do the leading on our own, to not share it with others, is both to reduce the quality of leadership offered, and to place ourselves in a dangerous position where we may not be supported and accountable in the ways that help keep us in a healthy place.

The minister does have some unique responsibilities

Fourthly, it is about a shared, kingdom-honouring goal. Leading well with others is not about us simply having a fun time together, important as that might be. There is a bigger picture, a bigger cause we are gathering around. There is something about God's purposes in the world we want to coalesce around, to work together on, to move forward. One way of defining church leadership is mobilizing and ordering a community around the person of Jesus and the priorities of his kingdom. This is what we are about.

Who are We to Lead With?

At one level, everyone. As the body of Christ we are all in this together, so in a sense we are looking to include everyone as a potential influencer for the good of the kingdom. However, such a simple answer is not ultimately a sufficient explanation of who we lead with.

Typically, people argue that what one needs is a team with whom one shares leadership. Teams are then often pitted against groups or committees, with a clear spin on a team being a far more attractive proposition than inviting someone to join a committee. For many years this was the approach I took, until my experience with the Arrow leaders began to show me how unhelpful this was.

Today I prefer to talk about leading well with others and how that can be done in a wide variety of groups, of which a team is just one type. 'Groups' is the generic term for a range of different gatherings of people. For example, within church life:

- Rota—group of people who exist to fulfil a task, for example the flower rota, or rota for reading the Scriptures.
- Club—group of people who gather because of a common interest or concern, for example the running club, senior citizens club.
- Support group—group of people who gather for mutual support/encouragement/development, for example the home group, bereavement group.
- Ministry group—group of people who together exercise a particular ministry task, for example the choir, music group, prayer ministry group.
- Committee—an elected group, normally with some statutory/legal constitution (or devolved from a wider group) with particular responsibilities, for example the fabric committee, finance committee.
- Team—a smaller, selected group focused on a particular task, for example Messy Church team.
- Council—an elected group, providing boundary keeping on the mission, policy formation and financial checks, normally with some statutory/legal constitution, for example the church council.

In different situations these groups may be defined and function in different ways, but the point is that there is a variety of groups. They are not better or worse than one another. What we need is to ensure they are fit for purpose—the right type of group for the purpose it is seeking to fulfil. For example, to create a committee for cleaning the church does not make sense. Nor does it make sense to run a support group for the bereaved as a team.

The advantage of this approach is that whatever situation we find ourselves in, we almost always have someone to lead well with. It may be an elder group or PCC, the finance committee or the leaders of the children's groups; perhaps the person who has faithfully prayed for the church and its health over many decades. Our job as a leader is to lead well with all these people and to seek to develop and nurture the leadership of each, so that they may grow in their capacity as a leader and in turn develop and nurture others in the same way.[18]

This will look different for the different types of groups, but it helps to know of any group:

- *Purpose*: why does the group exist? What is it trying to do? Then we can ask what is the best type of group to fulfil that purpose?
- *Structure*: what is the best way for the group to operate? How does it relate to other groups within the church or organisation?
- *Expectations*: what are the appropriate expectations for people to have about the group?

All groups benefit from clarity around these three areas, and it is one of the reasons why leaders constantly seek to help groups gain clarity around purpose, structure and expectations.

To Team or Not to Team

A team is one particular type of group, and when defined in a focused way (see endnote for one definition), it requires quite a lot of time and energy to function well.[19] Indeed, the literature on teams reminds us that a team is not a panacea, guaranteeing successful results, efficiency or great relationships.[20] In comparison to working as individuals or in other types of groups, working as a team can require the following from members:

- More time.
- More skill.
- More flexibility.
- More motivation.
- More emotional and relational investment.

Working in a team comes at a cost. This said, teams can enable us to reap the benefits of superior outcomes through that unique combination of elements—in short, synergy. So, how do we decide when we really need a team? Teams are useful for tasks where…

- *Ownership of a goal (a common purpose) should be shared*. What are the key decisions that need to be made and owned by a team of decision-makers rather than by an individual leader?
- *There is complexity*. For example the complexity associated with discerning a new vision and strategy, or developing a new major initiative.

- *Creative problem-solving is key*. Where synergy between members is needed to create something new and/or unique.
- *Diversity is vital*. Do we need a range of opinions, knowledge bases, experiences, styles of doing things (personality) to arrive at the right solution?
- *Close, interdependent relationships are at the heart of the matter.* Are the problem and the solution actually about relationships and interdependency? How crucial are relationships to the success of the task?
- *Implementation is achieved through interdependent action*. Are individuals reliant on each other to be able to play their part?

I think that leadership of a local church is one of the tasks that requires a team. As previously described, it is complex and weighty. Not everyone will be in a position where developing a leadership team is immediately possible, and the good news is that we do not need a leadership team to lead well with others. However, working towards developing such a team over time is probably a wise thing for most church leaders to do. Remember, the smallest team is two people. Even if we are not working in a team as I have defined it, team-like behaviours (as outlined in the literature on teams) can often be applied across the wide variety of groups we seek to lead well with.

5 Fostering a Collaborative Culture

Injit arrived at his church excited about a sense of call to serve in that place.[21] A few days after he started as the minister a churchwarden took him aside to alert him to the forthcoming PCC meeting the next week. 'Oh really,' said Injit, 'What do I need to know?' 'It's toxic,' came the reply. Injit felt this was a little over the top but was grateful for the warning. After the PCC meeting he realized the churchwarden's description was scarily accurate. He returned home that night and prayerfully determined that things were going to change, that the PCC would become the best group its members had ever belonged to.

Over the next three years he worked hard at creating a collaborative culture on the PCC, clear that this was the group he was going to have to lead well with. It was not easy, and there was much heartache along the way. Some people stepped down, others were eventually asked to leave. After three years the PCC was approaching the Annual Parochial Church Meeting, and once again there were tears amongst the members. But on this occasion not of hurt, frustration and anger as previously, but tears of sadness from several members who were having to step down as their term of service came to an end. They did not want to leave, because it had become the best group they belonged to; fun, focused, faith-filled and fruitful in what it did.[22]

So, what did Injit do over those three years? What can we do to foster a collaborative environment where we can lead well with others?

Ten Ideas

1 Embrace a Jesus-like Philosophy

Reading through the gospel accounts it is interesting to note how much time Jesus spent with relatively few people. Out of the crowds, there was the 72 (Luke 10.24). Out of the 72, there was the 12 (Mark 3.7–19). Out of the 12, there was the three (Mark 9.2). Early in my ordained ministry someone summarized this approach as, 'For the sake of many, invest in a few.' This does not mean we ignore everyone else. Jesus did not. But it does mean that we direct our energies towards a few people to help them develop as leaders. Such an approach may be controversial. Some may accuse us of having favourites. Some may question our choices (it is wise wherever possible to make such choices with others). But as a philosophy to embrace, I suggest it is vital if we are to lead well with others.

2 Engage others

Talk through with whoever is appropriate (deacon, elders, churchwarden, PCC, lay minister, superintendent) an approach to leading well with others. Explain why it is important, both theologically and pragmatically. Explore what it might look like and determine an agreed way forward with clear markers of progress. Talking it through with others has a number of advantages. (a) We are modelling what we are talking about. (b) We are likely to come up with a wiser plan with their input. (c) We create shared ownership of the way forward, with hopefully some support and encouragement to ensure it happens. What if we really cannot find anyone to talk things through with? We still, for the sake of many. invest in a few.

3 Pray and Teach

Injit committed to praying for the development of other leaders and the sharing of leadership. He was intentional in his praying, listening to the prompt of God. He taught about the nature of the church as a body where all are called to ministry, about his role as the minister and about the direction God was leading them. But he did not do those things once; he did them consistently over a significant period of time to begin to embed in the culture the development of leaders as a priority.

4 Model It

One of the main ways that people catch things is to see them in action. Another great leadership axiom is, 'If it is possible, take someone with you.' Rather than doing things on your own, if it is possible (and it is not always possible) draw someone alongside you to do it with you. For example:

- *Preparing to lead a family service*: who could we invite to join us in planning the service, perhaps delivering an aspect of it?
- *Preparing a sermon for a neighbouring church*: who could we invite to join us in the preparation process, perhaps delivering a small part of it?
- *Preparing for an important meeting:* who could we invite to join us in outlining the meeting, perhaps chairing one item?
- *Visiting a baptism couple*: who could we invite to come along with us and perhaps share their story of how they came to faith?
- *Planning an overhaul of the home groups*: who could we invite to join us for a morning to think and pray together about the best way forward?

It helps to draw into our world as diverse a group of people as possible. This has a long-term benefit. One of the problems of being a solo leader is that people who are not like us look at us and think, 'I'm not like them, I can't be a leader.' Whereas when we have a diversity of people leading, people can look at us and think, 'I'm not like them, but I am like N, so perhaps I could be a leader.' The importance of this really struck me when talking to an ordained woman from a BAME background. She explained that she grew up in a church where only white people were up front. It was not until a black woman came and preached at her church when she was an older teenager that she realized it was possible that she too could be a minister. Some years later, she was.

As we model this approach, we will also want to encourage others to take a similar approach. In this way the pattern of taking someone with us ripples out into the life of the church. A home group leader is always on the lookout for someone to draw into the leading of the home group. So too for the youth, children, choir, outreach project, CAP course or prayer team leaders.

5 Think 'Identify, Invest, Entrust'

In Mark 3.13–19 we see Jesus *identifying* the 12, those he is going to *invest* in (and later, beyond them, a wider group of women and men), and then over the next few chapters we see how he begins to *entrust* them with responsibility.

Of the three, identifying is probably the most difficult one to get right. It is also perhaps the most important. Why? Because we have to live with our choices. Taking time to pray, consult with others and approach people carefully is time well spent. It can be helpful to discuss with others what we are looking for in those who are going to share leadership, perhaps identifying a common set of values and a clear definition that provides a template against which to assess people's suitability. Obviously, setting the bar too high means no one is suitable, but setting the bar too low is also problematic. Leaders have oversight of other people, and if someone is not a safe person to follow they can do considerable damage to others. Work out where the bar is for you in your context and for the role you are discussing.[23]

Jesus invites the apostles 'to be with him.' Leadership is primarily learnt through relationship. Hence in the drawing others alongside us described above, it is as much about building relationship with other people as it is about getting a task done. Sharing life together, building relationship, journeying through the ups and downs, struggles and joys, are all a part of investing in leaders. There is a variety of ways we can do this, including social time with one another, simply getting to know each other's stories, enjoying each other's company. Also, there is the use of psychometric inventories which help us understand each other's preferences better and how they impact our working together.[24]

Jesus also entrusted them with responsibility. Ultimately it is in the doing of leadership that we learn about leadership. Giving people appropriate responsibility stretches people, and in the stretch there is growth.[25]

6 Create a Safe Space

Without safety, people hold back. Without safety, trust does not build. In order to change the PCC into a safe space, Injit needed to establish some ground rules quickly for how it should operate. He invited the group to reflect on what they liked about being part of the PCC and what could be improved. The group quickly identified a range of things they did not like, as well as a few things they did, and then began to make some ground rules for how they would behave to embrace the positive and prevent the negative. Each member was encouraged to uphold these ground rules, and to challenge others when they did not. Over time, as the group learnt to respect and listen to each other, it became a safer space for people to contribute, disagree, ask tough questions.

With safety, trust builds. With trust, you can begin to have healthy disagreement. With healthy disagreement, you can begin to make wiser decisions. With wiser decisions, you can gain a sense of being a part of something. With a sense of belonging, you can begin to build momentum. It all starts with a safe space. Healthy disagreement is vital for creative and effective collaborative leadership. However, it can take time to get there; Christian groups often struggle to do conflict well, mistakenly believing that conflict is to be avoided at all costs.

7 Aim for Round Pegs in Round Holes

Most churches have someone who is a square peg in a round hole. This may be for a variety of reasons. They may have once been a round peg in a round hole: either they have changed (for example, become stuck and need a new challenge; stale and in need of an injection of vision; developed new interests; or simply no longer having the time), or the hole has changed (for example, the role is no longer needed, or what is required has changed). They may never have been a round peg in a round hole, but generously took on the role to fill a gap or, less generously, to gain power. Being the wrong shape for the hole may be related to a character issue as much as a competency one.

Leaving square pegs in round holes is not good for anyone

Often square pegs in round holes are allowed to continue for quite a while. No one wants to upset them, perhaps because they have been so faithful in service. No one wants to challenge them, perhaps because they are known for their explosive temper. No one wants to see them leave, perhaps because there is no one else to take on this vital role.

But leaving square pegs in round holes is not good for anyone. It is not good for the person, as they are either not really enjoying what they are doing, or because they are being allowed to get away with behaviour that does not help them grow in godliness. It is not good for those they lead, who are either under someone who is not really very good in the role they exercise, or because they are being submitted to inappropriate behaviour. Tough as it is, tackling square pegs in round holes is a key leadership task. It is best done lovingly, sensitively, patiently and gently. Sometimes it needs to be done with the knowledge of those who have oversight of us and with other people present. But it does need to be done. It is one of the ways we foster a climate of collaboration, where people are encouraged to grow and develop and are appropriately held to account. If square pegs are left in round holes for too long people begin to assume it does not matter what you do or how you behave.

8 Cultivate a Flexible Leadership Style

Different people will need different approaches to help them grow into leadership. Really talented managers of rugby teams do not treat all their squad members in the same way. They know that one will be motivated by lots of encouragement, another needs straight talking. One needs some down time away from the crowd, another finds solitude isolating and draining. One person likes feedback straight after the game, another needs some space between the game and feedback. Good managers change their approach in order for every team member to play their best game.

It involves getting to know our people well, and the best way to do this is, once again, to ask questions. What motivates you? What de-energizes you? How do you like to receive encouragement? What is the best way for me to give you feedback? Where are you feeling challenged at the moment? What does stretch look like for you?

The mistake is to assume that how we do things, or how we like things, is the way others will. Be flexible.

9 Nurture Mutual Support

One day we will move on, and if everything has been channelled through us things will not be in the best place to continue after we leave. Part of fostering a collaborative culture in which we learn to lead well with others is helping people support one another. In his excellent Grove booklet, *Refusing to be Indispensable,* Andy Griffiths outlines a radical approach to ensuring this happened in churches he led. He took the decision that he would not visit anyone in their home for pastoral reasons for a year, and instead he encouraged mutual support amongst the congregation members.[26] Ultimately, we are trying to do ourselves out of a job and develop the leadership so that they can support and care for one another without us being present.

10 Blend Task, Individual and Group

In the 1960s John Adair developed a model for working with groups of people where he suggested that for every group there is a combination of a task that needs to be achieved (the reason why the group exists), a group dynamic that needs to be cultivated (ensuring the group is a safe space and functions well), and individuals who need to be nurtured (cared for and developed to become all God made them to be). A good leader ensures that attention is given to all three elements in any group they lead.

Most of us are wired with a predisposition to focus on one of these aspects. I am task focused; I like to get things done. In any group I lead, the danger is that I will focus on the task aspect of the group to the neglect of the other two. Others will be more individually focused, concerned about people and how they are getting on, feeling, responding to what is happening. Some may be more wired to the group dynamic, thinking about how the whole is working, or not.

Not sure which you are? Ask yourself, which of these am I likely to default to under pressure: getting the job done, caring for an individual person, maintaining harmony and healthy functioning within the group? Still not sure? Ask someone who knows you well or has worked with you in the past.

Once we know our likely default, it means we can do two things to ensure all three aspects of good group working are maintained: (a) We can work a little harder at the things that do not come so naturally. (b) We can appoint others to the group who bring what we do not naturally bring. Ultimately, as the group leader, it is part of my role to ensure all three things are blended well in any group I lead, because these aspects of a group all need to function well for healthy collaboration to occur.

A Way Forward

These ten ideas are not the only things that one can do to help foster a collaborative culture, but they are a good start. Practised consistently over time, they will go a long way to creating an environment in which others are developed as leaders, and those already in leadership are nurtured to bring their best to their role.

It is what Injit did, and the PCC became a healthy and thriving group with which he was able to lead well. Ultimately that rippled out into the church's life as a whole. As the PCC exercised leadership, the congregation began to grow in worship of God, in fellowship with one another and in mission to the community they served and the wider world beyond. That is what can happen when we lead well with others. We must note, though, that it did not happen overnight for Injit, and it did not start with anything very big. The reality is that most of us have little free capacity for bringing about change, but we do have some. So, we start where we are, and identify one simple step forward. It might be to break up the PCC into small groups of three to discuss one item on the agenda, thus giving a voice to people who so far have rarely, if ever, contributed to the group as a whole. It might be to invite someone to share their story of coming to faith as part of our sermon one Sunday. It might be to visit someone in their place of work and ask them to share their insights and challenges on leadership in their context. All these are steps towards a more collaborative approach to leadership, and simple, small steps over time can get us a long way.

Most of us have little free capacity for bringing about change, but we do have some

6 Epilogue

Which do you want to be? Sally or Injit?

Remember Sally sinking under the weight of responsibility and expectation—dedicated, loyal, visionary, capable…and burnt out.

Remember Injit, committed to finding a way of turning a toxic group into a group he could lead well with—dedicated, loyal, visionary, capable…and surviving (perhaps even thriving).

The challenge is that Injit's route takes more time and energy.

We all know it is far quicker to do something ourselves than train someone else to do it alongside us. It is far easier to make a decision on our own than involve others in the process (and, even worse, the decision might not go our way). It is far simpler to avoid the difficult conversation with the square peg in the round hole than face a tough conversation that might not go well.

Quicker, easier, simpler. Why would we not choose this route?

Because at the end of it there may well be a burnt-out minister, an unhealthily dependent congregation, a lack of leaders, some unwise decisions and a church that is not fully fulfilling the missional potential God has for it.

There is a better way. But it is not quick, easy or simple. It is more likely to be slow, difficult and complex. Why would we choose this route?

Because at the end of it there may well be a thriving minister leading well with others, a healthier congregation, a bunch of leaders, some wiser decisions and a church that is more fully fulfilling the missional potential God has for it.

Time to choose.

Notes

1 Springboard was the Archbishops of Canterbury and York's initiative for evangelism during the 1990s.

2 An Anglican mission agency focused on the UK: www.cpas.org.uk

3 The dates of these different generational groups are debated with no consensus. These dates seem to be the most commonly used.

4 See James Lawrence, *Engaging Gen Y* (Grove Leadership booklet L8).

5 Adapted from Jimmy Long, *The Leadership Jump* (Downers Grove, IL: IVP, 2009).

6 See Emma Sykes, *Vulnerability in Leadership* (Grove Leadership booklet L24).

7 See Patrick Lencioni, *The Advantage* (Hoboken, NJ: John Wiley, 2012) for an excellent overview of how to shape a healthy culture and why it is so important.

8 For more on this see David Robertson, *Collaborative Ministry* (Abingdon: BRF, 2007) chapter 4.

9 He also suggested that overall perhaps clergy lack courage, the courage needed to bring about necessary change in the light of inevitable opposition.

10 Based on the experience of an actual clergy person, name changed.

11 Or 'ministry,' same root word.

12 Gilbert Bilezikian, *Community 101* (Grand Rapids, MI: Zondervan, 1997) p 131.

13 Love one another, forgive one another, carry one another's burdens and so on.

14 Gordon Fee, *Listening to the Spirit in the Text* (Grand Rapids, MI: Eerdmans, 2000) p 124.

15 See Tom Rath and Barrie Conchie, *Strengths Based Leadership* (New York: Gallup Press, 2009).

16 Leadership of a school and leadership of a political party were the other two (source lost).

17 There are other key things Christian leaders give their attention to, most important of which is modelling themselves on Jesus, and then discerning direction, enabling action, developing leaders, shaping culture, facilitating communication.

18 See the *Growing Leaders* courses at www.cpas.org.uk/growingleaders as a way of facilitating leadership development in a church.

19 One way to define a Christian team is a 'number of interdependent people committed to a common purpose, who choose to co-operate in order to achieve exceptional results for the glory of God.'

20 The following are my go-to books on teams: Patrick Lencioni, *The Five Dysfunctions of a Team* (Hoboken, NJ: John Wiley, 2002); Patrick Lencioni, *The Ideal Team Player* (Hoboken, NJ: John Wiley, 2016); Pat Macmillan, *The Performance Factor* (Nashville, TN: Broadman and Holman, 2001); Ryan Hartwig and Warren Bird, *Teams That Thrive* (Downers Grove, IL: IVP, 2015).

21 Again based on an actual vicar, name changed.

22 For more on the twelve common dysfunctions of PCCs and what to do about them see James Lawrence, *PCC Tonight* (Coventry: CPAS, 2016).

23 There are several lists that help shape the qualities we look for: Acts 6.2–4; 1 Tim 3.1–13; Titus 1.5–9.

24 For example Myers Briggs, Enneagram, Interpersonal Style, Gilmore Fraleigh.

25 For more on this see James Lawrence, *Growing Leaders* (Abingdon: BRF/CPAS, 2020).

26 Andy Griffiths, *Refusing to be Indispensable: Vacating the Centre of Church Life* (Grove Leadership booklet L31). Do get hold of this booklet to get a sense of the context for this decision and the fascinating outcomes that followed.